D1567259

Sabine Lohf

Building Your Own Toys

Sabine Lohf

Building Your Own Toys

In this book
you will find
many great
things you can
make yourself.

℗ CHILDRENS PRESS®
CHICAGO

Translation by Mrs. Werner Lippmann and Mrs. Ruth Bookey

Library of Congress Cataloging-in-Publication Data

Lohf, Sabine.
    [Ich bau mir was zum Spielen. English]
    Building your own toys / by Sabine Lohf.
      p. cm.
    Translation of: Ich bau mir was zum Spielen.
    Summary: Provides instructions on how to make simple toys and
games.
    ISBN 0-516-09251-0
    1. Toy making—Juvenile literature.   2. Games—Juvenile
literature.   3. Handicraft—Juvenile literature.   [1. Toy making.
2. Games.   3. Handicraft]   I. Title.
TT174.L6413   1989
745.592—dc20
                                        89-22276
                                           CIP
                                            AC

Published in the United States in 1990 by Childrens Press®, Inc.,
5440 North Cumberland Avenue, Chicago, IL 60656.

This book is based on contributions published in the German
magazine *Spielen Und Lernen* © Velber Verlag GmbH, Seelze,
F.R.G. This collection was originally published under the title *Ich
Bau Mir Was Zum Spielen,* copyright © 1986 by Ravensburger
Buchverlag Otto Maier GmbH, English translation copyright ©
1990 by Ravensburger Buchverlag Otto Maier GmbH, West
Germany.

Contents

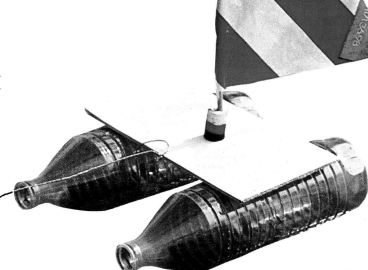

Front Loader

You will need:

1 big box
2 small boxes
3 cardboard tubes
2 strips corrugated cardboard
2 strips cardboard
½ big round cardboard oatmeal box
1 toilet-paper tube
  glue
4 straight pins with glass
  tops
paint and paintbrushes

1. First glue the 2 small boxes on top of the big box. Glue the toilet-paper tube upright in front of the small boxes.

2. Then glue the cardboard tubes under the big box. The ends of the tubes must stick out from under the box on both sides.

3. Put the corrugated strips around the tubes and glue the ends together to make "tracks."

4. Stick the oatmeal-carton half between two cardboard strips with pins so that it is movable. Use 2 more pins to attach cardboard strips to the front of the big box. Then the shovel can move up and down.

Glue on a toilet-paper tube chimney.

The shovel moves up and down.

straight pin

5. Paint the front loader with bright colors.

Tom and Harry

You will need:

Paper, cardboard, string, scissors, two-sided clear tape,
4 balloons

1. First blow up 2
   balloons and knot them
   together. You need a
   big balloon for the body
   and a smaller one for
   the head.

2. With a long string, knot
   the balloons together.
   Let a piece of string
   hang out.

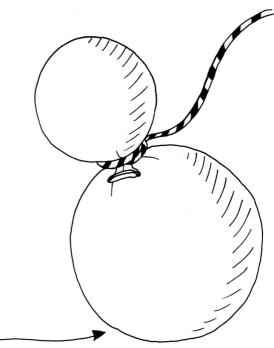

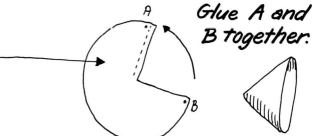

3. Cut the flat feet for Tom and
   Harry from cardboard and
   tape them under the bigger
   balloons.

4. For noses, either cut a
   piece of paper as the
   drawing shows, or fold a
   little paper hat and tape
   it to the balloon.
   Wings and ears can also be cut from paper and stuck to
   the balloons with tape. Tie a string around the neck. When
   you pull up on Tom and Harry with the long strings, they
   will always land on their feet!

Feed the Bulldogs

<u>You will need:</u>

3 empty coffee cans, brown wrapping paper, glue, cardboard, scissors, some red construction paper, paint and paintbrushes, some balls or marbles to play the game

1. Cut out 3 cardboard head halves, as shown. Cut sharp teeth too!

Put glue here and attach to can.

Leg

Tail

2. Cut 3 tails and 6 legs out of cardboard. Cut 3 tongues out of red construction paper.

3. Then wrap the wrapping paper around the coffee can and glue the paper to the can.

4. Heads, tails, and legs will also be glued to the cans. Glue the tongue to the can as shown.

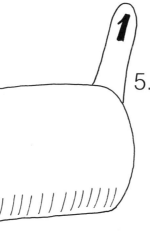

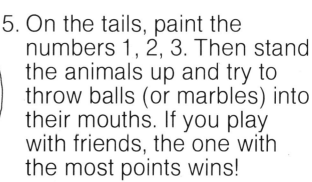

5. On the tails, paint the numbers 1, 2, 3. Then stand the animals up and try to throw balls (or marbles) into their mouths. If you play with friends, the one with the most points wins!

A Little Harbor

You will need:

1 big piece of cardboard to hold many boxes of different sizes, glue, some lighter cardboard, corrugated paper, scissors, felt-tip markers, poster paints, empty boxes and plastic tubs, little wooden sticks, milk cartons, water for the boats, some clay, paper, paints and paintbrushes

1. Glue different-size boxes to the big piece of cardboard.

2. Cut roofs out of corrugated paper and glue them to the "houses" as shown. Then paint all your houses. Let the paint dry.

3. Draw windows and doors with felt-tip markers.

Glue on the roof like this.

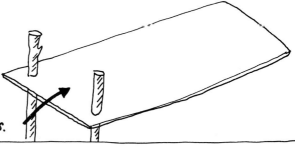

Clay

4. You can make boats out of empty margarine tubs. Place a bit of clay in the middle of each tub. Push a little wooden stick with a paper sail into the clay. (You could also fold some paper boats, but they sink too fast!)

5. Now take your "harbor" to a little pond, the beach, or even a puddle! Place the boats in the water and have a good time!

You can also build a wharf with a piece of cardboard and some sticks.

The Dancing Ghost

You will need:

Some old white curtains or cloth remnants, 2 buttons, cotton balls, needle and thread, white yarn, old costume jewelry, glue, felt-tip markers

1. Crumple the cotton balls into one large ball.

2. Put a piece of the material over the large ball. Make sure it is a large piece that hangs down on all sides.

3. Tie the material together under the ball tightly so that it makes a neck for your ghost.

4. Tie a long strip of material around the "neck." Make sure it hangs down on both sides.

5. Tie knots at each end of the long strip, and there are your ghost's arms!

6. Now decorate your ghost with old costume jewelry, and glue on buttons for eyes. Draw the rest of the face with markers.

7. Now sew strings onto the top of the head and on the knot in each arm. If you hold these strings in your hands, you can make your ghost dance!

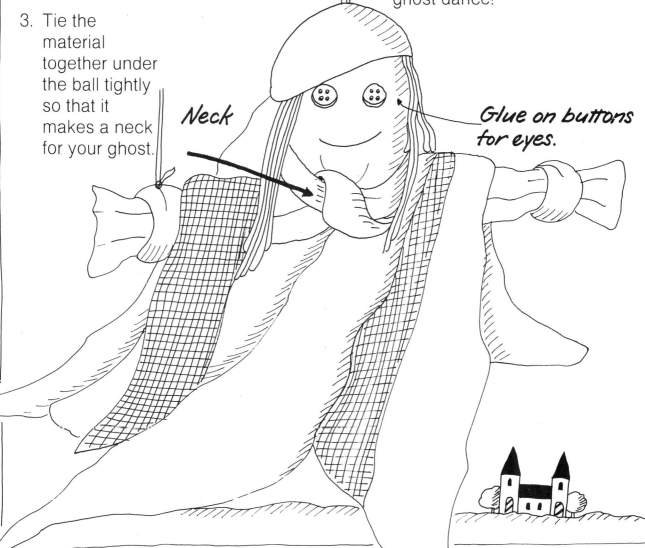

Neck

Glue on buttons for eyes.

14

Red Fire Engine

You will need:

1 big box, 1 small box, 1 cardboard tube from a roll of toilet paper, cardboard, glue, scissors, brass paper fasteners, paints and brushes

The small box is the driver's cab.

1. Glue the small box on top of the large box. The small box is the cab of the truck.

2. Behind the small box, glue the cardboard tube.

You can move the ladder up and down.

3. The ladder can be made from 2 long cardboard strips and 5 smaller strips; glue the smaller strips as shown in the picture.

4. The finished ladder is "hooked" between 2 cardboard strips that have been bent and glued onto the back of the big box (see the picture). To hook the ladder, use two brass fasteners.

5. Cut out 4 wheels and glue them onto the large box (see the picture). If you want the wheels to turn, use a brass fastener to attach each wheel to the box.

6. So that the fire engine will look authentic, you must paint it red.

Crepe-Paper Dolls

You will need:

Newspapers, clear tape, crepe paper, glue, wood excelsior, poster paint, brushes

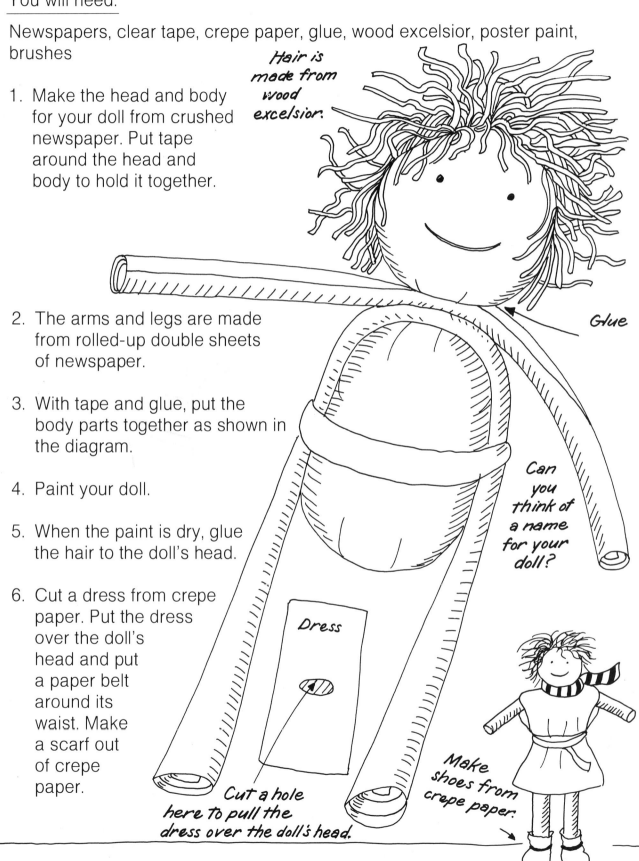

Hair is made from wood excelsior.

1. Make the head and body for your doll from crushed newspaper. Put tape around the head and body to hold it together.

Glue

2. The arms and legs are made from rolled-up double sheets of newspaper.

3. With tape and glue, put the body parts together as shown in the diagram.

4. Paint your doll.

Can you think of a name for your doll?

5. When the paint is dry, glue the hair to the doll's head.

6. Cut a dress from crepe paper. Put the dress over the doll's head and put a paper belt around its waist. Make a scarf out of crepe paper.

Dress

Cut a hole here to pull the dress over the doll's head.

Make shoes from crepe paper.

18

Plaster Castle

I'd like to live here.

You will need:

2 cardboard tubes, cardboard, glue, some small stones, plaster of paris, a plastic bowl, a stick to stir the plaster, water, poster paints, snail shells

Glue on painted roofs made from cardboard.

1. On a big solid piece of cardboard, glue the two cardboard rolls and a couple of sturdy cardboard walls.

2. While the glue is drying, mix the plaster in the bowl according to package directions.

3. Now smear the plaster on the cardboard walls. Pile up stones against the walls.

Alternate a layer of stones, some plaster, etc. Stick on some snail shells.

4. The two towers and their roofs also get a layer of plaster. Then stick on a few stones here and there. Let the castle dry thoroughly. When it is dry, you can paint it in wonderful colors.

While the plaster or the paint is drying, you might make a couple of stone-and-plaster monsters.

Owl Mask

<u>You will need:</u>

Heavy construction paper (in different colors), crepe paper, scissors, glue, string

1. Draw the outline of an owl's head on the construction paper and cut it out.

2. Cut out yellow eyes and a black beak, and glue them to the head.

3. From paper and crepe paper, tear lots of long strips and glue them to the back of the owl's head.

4. If you want to wear the owl as a mask, you have to attach a string to each side of the head, as shown. Cut holes in the eyes so you can see through it!

The paper strips make a nice swishing sound as you walk around in your owl mask.

Birds and Planes

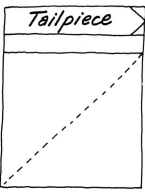

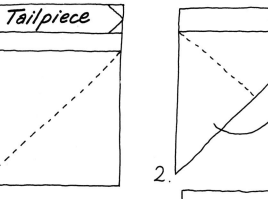

1. Fold a rectangular piece of colored or white paper at the dotted line. Cut off half of the remaining paper for a tail (see picture 1).

2. Fold the paper again at the dotted line in picture 2.

3. Now you have a triangle with a little extra on top. Open your folded paper.

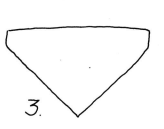

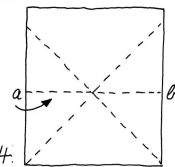

4. Bring together points A and B in picture 4.

5. Fold corners C and D to points. (A and B will be in the center, as in picture 5.)

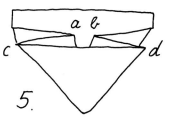

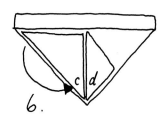

6. Fold points C and D down so that their tips meet at the bottom, as in picture 6.

7. Now fold C and D inward, as shown in picture 7.

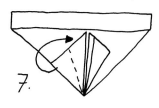

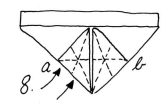

8. Fold points A and B in picture 8 toward the center.

9. Open the last folds you made.

10. Bend the point of the triangle under at the dotted line in picture 10. Then open the folds and pull down the center to make a point.

11. Now glue the tailpiece under the wings, as shown in the pictures.

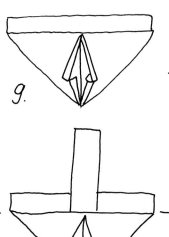

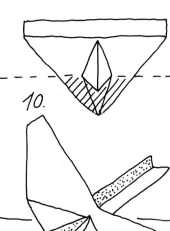

12. Picture 12 shows what the plane looks like from the top.

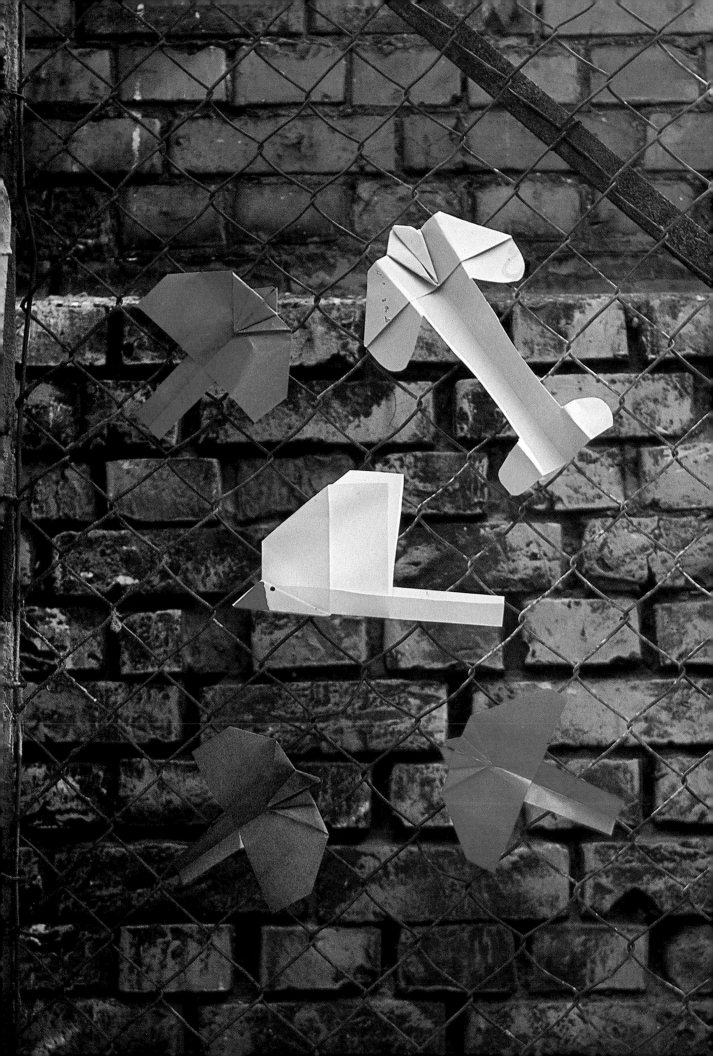

Magician's Hat

You will need:

2 big sheets of sturdy colored paper, glue, scissors, some gold stars, crepe paper for decoration

Roll up.

1. Roll one of the sheets of paper into a pointed hat. (The opening on the bottom must be big enough to fit your head.)

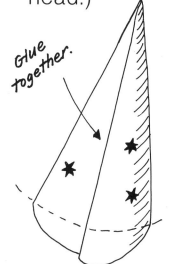

Glue together.

2. Cut a big circle from the second sheet of paper. That will be the brim of the hat.

3. In the middle of the circle, cut another circle, a little smaller than the opening of your pointed hat.

4. Cut around the inner circle of the brim as the diagram shows.

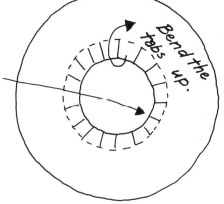

Bend the tabs up.

5. Bend the cut tabs up. Put glue on them and stick them to the pointed hat.

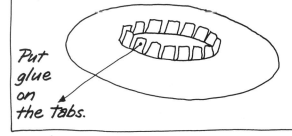

Put glue on the tabs.

Finally, glue the stars on the hat. Wind a crepe-paper ribbon and bow around your hat. Now you are ready to do some magic!

Papier-Mâché Duck

You will need:

2 balloons, old newspapers, papier-mâché paste, a plastic bowl, a stick to stir the paste, glue, red or orange construction paper, paint and a paintbrush, a string, stones

1. Mix the paste with water in the bowl, as instructed on the package.

2. Then blow up the balloons, one big and one smaller.

Head

Body

3. Tear the newspaper into strips, dip the strips into the paste, and wrap them around the balloons.

The bill is made from construction paper.

4. Now you have to wait about 2 days until the paper is hard and dry. Then cut a hole in the "body" where you will later glue on the head. Dribble a little paste in the opening and then fill the "belly" with stones. (This way the duck can never tip over.)

5. Glue the head onto the hole. Finally, paint your duck with waterproof paint. Attach the string. Now you can take it swimming! Oh, yes. Don't forget to cut a bill from red or orange construction paper and glue it to the head.

Dolls' Costume Party

How about having a costume party for your dolls? You can dress them up for the big event with things you probably have around the house— newspapers, glue, yarn, odds and ends of cloth, crepe paper, light cardboard, construction paper,

party streamers.
Cut doll clothes from
crepe paper or cloth.
Glue the seams
together. You can
make paper hats. Big

pointy noses or
masks are easy to
make from cardboard
or construction
paper.

White Mice

You will need:

Hard-boiled eggs, scissors, white paper, glue, a ball of yarn, pins with black glass heads

1. Cut a half-circle out of the white paper. Glue the circle together to form a pointed nose.

2. Cut some ears out of white paper.

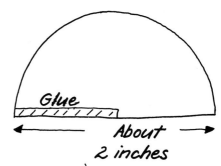

Glue

About 2 inches

If the nose doesn't fit the egg, trim off a little at the back.

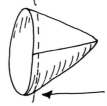

Bend each ear as shown, apply some glue to the bent part, and stick it on the egg.

3. Glue the ears and nose to the hard-boiled egg.

4. Glue a few yarn whiskers on the nose.

5. Of course, the mouse needs a nice long yarn tail.

6. Then, very carefully, stick two pins into the egg for eyes.

Ferryboat

I'll go for a ride!

You will need:

1 big rectangular box, 1 small rectangular box, 1 very small box, cardboard, scissors, some string, glue, poster paints, a brush, some toothpicks, clear tape, shellac in a spray can, cardboard tubes from toilet-paper rolls

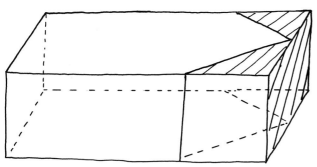

1. From the big box, cut out the areas that are striped in the diagram.

2. Put glue on the edges and press them together. Also put tape over the edges.

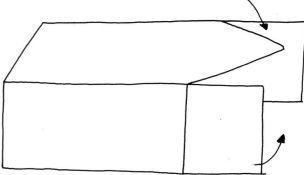
Glue

3. The diagram shows how the small box is glued to the big one.

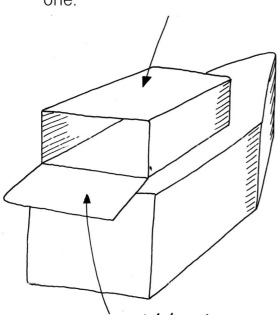
It would be nice if the small box had a flap for unloading.

4. Now the ship needs smokestacks and a little cabin for the captain. Use the smallest box for the captain's cabin, and cardboard tubes for the smokestacks.

5. A railing can be cut from cardboard, or you can stick toothpicks into the edge of the ship and connect them with string and glue. Put a little flag on your ferryboat, too.

6. The last thing to do is paint your ship in bright colors. If you want it to last longer, spray the bottom of your ferry with shellac. Ship ahoy!

Sand Games

You will need:

Marbles, toothpicks, felt-tip markers, scissors, sticks, colored paper, stones

Who will reach the black dot first?

Entrance

LABYRINTH (picture at right)

Collect lots of little sticks and break them into even smaller pieces. Then make a labyrinth in the sand, as shown in the picture on the right. Or make a different kind of labyrinth, as shown in the diagram at left. How do you get to the black dot in the middle?

FLAG GAME

Cut little flags out of paper. Put a number on each flag. Put toothpicks through the flags and stick them in the sand. From a distance of one foot, try to hit the flags with a marble.

Goal

WHO WILL REACH THE CENTER FIRST?

Draw circles in the sand with a stick, as shown in the diagram at left. Each player gets 2 little stones, one to hide, one to play with. Where did you hide your stone? Left? Right? The other player has to guess. If the guess is correct, the other player may advance one circle with his or her stone. If the guess is wrong, the stone must remain where it is. Now it's your turn to guess. Whoever reaches the center first wins.

How does the marble get into the snail shell?

A Summer Snowman

You will need:

2 balloons, newspapers, red and white paint, scissors, papier-mâché paste, crepe paper, clear tape, a few small stones, 1 carrot, a hat (or make your own hat out of black paper)

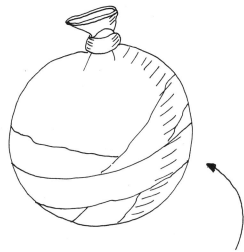

1. Blow up the balloons, one big and one smaller.

2. Mix the paste in a plastic bowl. Let it stand 10 minutes. Then stir it some more.

3. Tear the newspapers into strips.

4. Pull each newspaper strip through the paste and wrap it around the balloons. (Make 3 layers of strips.)

5. The wrapped balloons must dry thoroughly.

6. Cut a hole in the bigger balloon (the "belly" of the snowman). Dribble some paste into the hole and drop in a few stones. (Now the snowman won't tip over!)

7. Glue the smaller balloon (the head) over the hole.

8. Stick a carrot on the snowman's face for a nose.

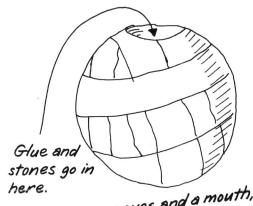

Glue and stones go in here.

Draw eyes and a mouth, and put a hat on your snowman.

Don't forget the scarf!

Sun Hat

You will need:

Newspapers, papier-mâché paste, clear tape, a plastic bowl, a stick, light cardboard, crepe paper, poster paint

1. Mix the paste in a bowl as described on the container.

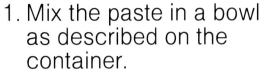

Stir well!

2. Crumple a few sheets of newspaper into a ball. The ball should be as large as your head.

3. Wrap the ball securely with tape.

4. Now you have to cut out a brim from light cardboard. Put the brim over the paper ball.

5. Now tear more newspapers into strips and dip each strip in the paste. Place the strips over the paper ball and brim.

Glue flowers on the brim.

6. The hat must dry thoroughly.

7. When the hat is dry, take the paper ball out of the hat.

8. Paint the hat. Cut some flowers from crepe paper and glue them on the hat. Make a bow from crepe paper and glue it on the hat.

Now you can wear your hat!

Giant's Head

You will need:

A big cardboard box, a broom, construction paper, glue, paint, crepe paper, cardboard tubes from toilet-paper rolls, scraps of colorful paper

✷ NOTE: The cardboard box must be big enough for a broom head to fit in it.

First you paint the box and glue the crepe-paper hair on the box.

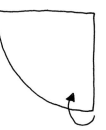

The bigger the nose you want, the bigger the quarter circle should be.

Cut a quarter circle out of construction paper, roll it into a cone, and glue it together.

When the head is done, find a large piece of cloth. The best thing would be a bed sheet. Hang the sheet over the head of the broom and stick the broom head into the box.

Hold the broomstick in your hand and hide under the sheet.

It will be very funny when you stick your hand out through the sheet!

Angela Wiesner/Foto: Sabine Lohf

Leo, the Rolling Lion

You will need:

A round plastic or cardboard container (perhaps a detergent bottle or oatmeal box); cardboard; 2 skewers; some heavier cardboard; yellow, brown, and red yarn; yellow and green poster paint; a brush; 1 red and 1 black felt-tip marker; string; scissors; glue

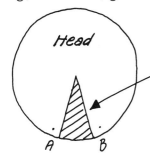

1. Cut out a circle from the cardboard. Cut a triangular piece out of the circle, as the diagram shows, and glue points A and B together.

2. Paint everything yellow—the head, the body, and the heavier cardboard (this will be made into wheels later).

3. Glue 2 long pieces of the lighter cardboard to the back of the head,

   and cut a hole in the round box (the body).

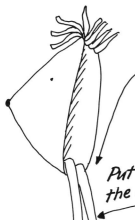

Put the cardboard strips through the hole, and glue them on.

Draw eyes and a mouth.

4. Cut four wheels from sturdy yellow-painted cardboard. Poke a hole in the middle of each wheel. Then mount the wheels on the skewers.

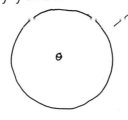

Stick the skewers through the body, put on the wheels, and wrap some red yarn around the ends of the skewers.

5. To make a tail, double a long piece of yellow yarn and wrap more yellow yarn around it. At the end, tie on a tassel of brown yarn.

6. Glue the tail on the body, put a bow around the lion's neck, and take him for a walk.

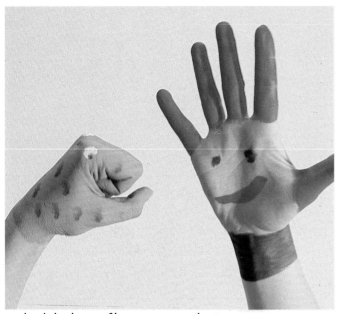

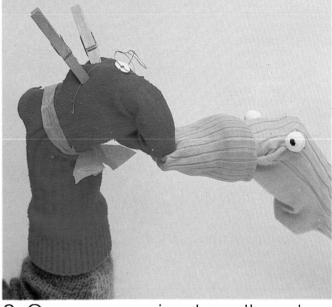

1. Using finger paints, you can turn your hands into frogs, little people, and many other characters. When you put your painted hands through the side holes of your TV, it will be very funny.

2. Or you can simply pull socks over your hands. You can create all sorts of characters using clothespins, wires, buttons, and anything else you can think of!

Things to Do With the TV

3. The man and the bird are cut from cardboard and painted. Glue long strips of cardboard to the backs of the heads. Hold the strips in your hands and let the two walk across your TV screen.

Box TV

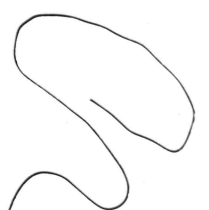

Find a large square cardboard box. Cut a big hole in it as shown. That will be the screen. In both the side walls and the top of your "TV" you have to cut holes large enough to allow your hands to fit through.

Paint your TV on the inside. Make a landscape from egg cartons. Put some of your toys in the landscape.

Other things to do with your TV are on the opposite page.

(Don't forget to glue buttons on your TV to turn it on and off.)

Flying Dragon

You will need:

A cardboard tube, colored construction paper, scissors, glue, a large rubber band, a long stick

1. Wrap and glue construction paper around the cardboard tube.

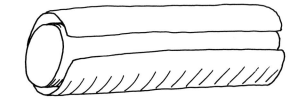

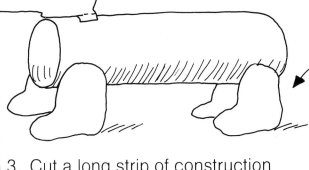

2. Cut a head and some feet out of construction paper and glue them to the tube.

3. Cut a long strip of construction paper. It must fit into the tube, but should be 8 inches longer than the tube.

4. Fold the strip over on the end and put the rubber band in the fold (as shown). Glue the strip inside the tube. Leave the rubber band hanging out at one end. Leave a "tail" hanging out the other end.

This is how to make the dragon fly: Slide the dragon's body over a long stick. Put the rubber band over the front of the stick (as shown in the photo). Stretch the rubber band by pulling gently on the paper strip that comes out of the back of the dragon. Let go of the strip, and the dragon will fly through the air. (CAUTION: Do not fly the dragon indoors. Never point it at your body or at another person.)

5. Tear strips of colored paper and glue them to the dragon's body.

Hobgoblin

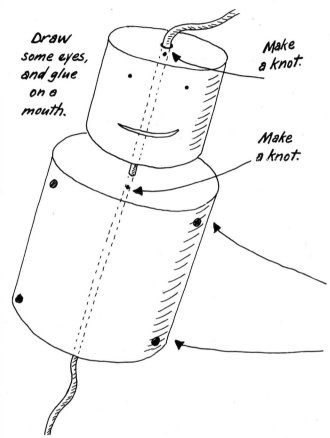

Three hobgoblins are really noisy!

You will need:

2 small cans, 2 larger cans, lots of bottle caps, string, hammer and nails, some wire, red paper, glue, bottle opener, some tissue paper, a felt-tip marker

Draw some eyes, and glue on a mouth.

Make a knot.

Make a knot.

1. Using a nail, hammer a hole into the bottoms of all 4 cans. (CAUTION: Be careful with the hammer and nail. Or have an adult do the hammering for you.)

2. Pull string through the holes, and make a big knot right at the holes.

3. Poke holes for arms and legs into the sides of the big cans. You can make the holes on the lower edges of the cans with a bottle opener.

4. Pound holes in the bottle caps and pull string through, for arms and legs.

5. When you think the arms and legs are long enough, knot them in the big can.

6. Make the hobgoblin a cape out of tissue paper or a piece of thin cloth.

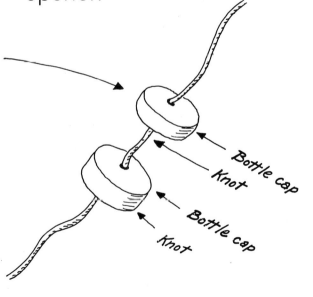

Bottle cap

Knot

Bottle cap

Knot

Felt Penguin

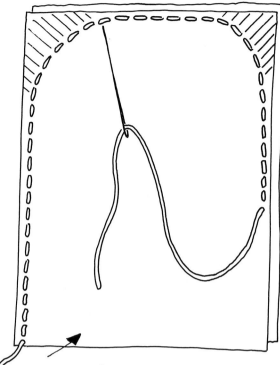

You will need:

4 pieces of felt (2 white, 1 black, and 1 yellow), needle and thread, scissors, some cardboard, glue, 2 buttons, some cotton batting

1. Put the two pieces of white felt together, cut off the edges (as indicated by the striped area in the diagram), and sew the two pieces together.

2. When you have stuffed the cotton into the body, sew the 2 pieces of white felt together on the bottom.

Leave this edge open until you've stuffed in the cotton!

3. Out of the black felt, cut two wings and a piece for the head, as indicated in the diagram. Glue the head piece and wings right on the body. Sew on the buttons for eyes.

4. For the beak and feet, use yellow felt. Use 4 layers of felt, glued together, for the beak. The feet will be stronger if you glue them to a piece of cardboard (that's the same shape), then glue the feet on the body.

Head piece

Beak

Wings

Egg Stand

<u>You will need:</u>

One egg carton, 2 skewers, some cardboard, red and yellow paper, glue, 2 empty toilet-paper tubes, some yarn, crepe paper in different colors, needle, thread, 8 hard-boiled eggs

1. Cut the egg carton in half so you have 6 places for eggs (or perhaps you will be able to find a 6-egg carton). Cut off the lid of the carton.

2. Cut a roof out of cardboard and glue red and yellow paper strips on it. Bend the front edge down. The roof should be as wide as the egg carton.

3. At the ends of the roof, poke holes for skewers. Also make holes in the egg carton so your skewers will stay securely in place. Put 6 hard-boiled eggs into the carton.

4. Make salespeople from the toilet-paper tubes. Stick a hard-boiled egg in each tube.

5. Draw faces on the eggs, glue some yarn hair on the woman, and make a paper cap for the man. Make a crepe-paper dress for the woman.

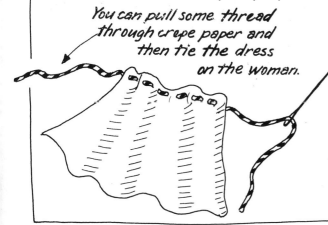

You can pull some thread through crepe paper and then tie the dress on the woman.

Simply wrap the man in crepe paper and attach it with glue. Make paper rolls for arms and glue them to the bodies.

Fresh
Eggs

Rustling Bears

You will need:

A piece of white material, a piece of brown material, glue, newspapers, brown kraft paper, some yarn, 4 buttons, some ribbon, felt-tip markers

My tummy is full of newspaper, and when you squeeze me, I'll crackle!

1. Fold the cloth in two on a table and sew it closed on the side, as shown.

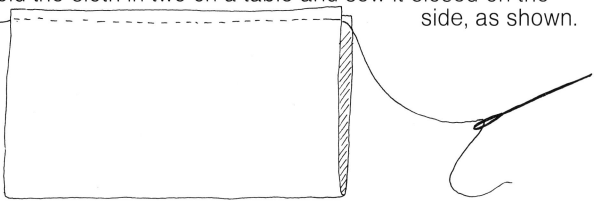

2. Crumple up newspaper and stuff it into the piece of material. Put more paper at the end where the bear's belly will be.

3. Sew both ends of the material piece shut .

4. Tie a ribbon around your bear to form a head.

5. Cut arms, legs, and ears out of newspaper or kraft paper, and glue them on the body. Sew on button eyes and glue on some yarn whiskers. Draw a mouth.

The bear's nose is made from a piece of toilet-paper tube.

Sailboat

For a mouse sailboat, I'll have to cut a smaller sail.

You will need:

2 empty plastic bottles,
1 small wooden board,
1 cork, a round wooden stick, a colorful plastic bag, glue, scissors, some paint,
1 tack or a small nail

1. Cut a triangular sail from the plastic bag as shown.

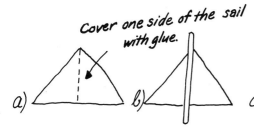

Cover one side of the sail with glue.

a)   b)   c)

2. Open the triangle and put glue on point B. Lay the wooden stick on the fold line and fold the sail back together.

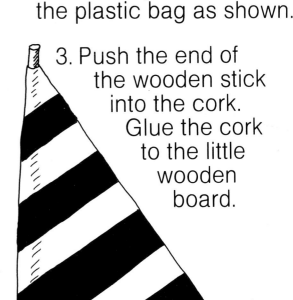

3. Push the end of the wooden stick into the cork. Glue the cork to the little wooden board.

4. Glue the plastic bottles to the underside of the board, about 3½ inches apart, or so that the board hangs over on the sides a little bit.

5. Finally, tack or nail a string to the board.

A Colorful Train

You will need:

A big round plastic or cardboard container, sturdy cardboard, 2 empty toilet-paper tubes, different-size boxes, construction paper in different colors, 4 wooden sticks, glue, scissors, clear tape, poster paints

1. Glue together the round container and some boxes, and you have an engine.

2. Make a passenger car out of a larger box.

3. Draw 6 circles, all the same size, on cardboard and cut them out.

4. Make a hole in the middle of each circle to put the wooden sticks through.

5. Put 2 sticks through the lower part of the engine, and 1 stick through the passenger car. Each stick should extend about 1½ inches beyond the boxes.

6. Put the wheels on the sticks. Wrap the ends of the sticks a few times with clear tape. The wheels should turn easily, but shouldn't fall off.

7. Use the fourth stick to connect the passenger car to the engine. Finally, paint your train.

Blow-Away "Fliers"

You will need:

Lightweight cardboard, white drawing paper, tracing paper, ruler, pencil, scissors, glue

You can make all kinds of fliers.

4 inches

1. On the cardboard, draw a square about 4" x 4".

2. Cut out the square, roll it up, and glue it together.

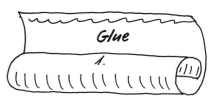

Glue 1.

3 inches

4½ inches

3. Cut a rectangle 3" x 4½" out of the cardboard. Roll it up and glue it. It should be larger in diameter than the first roll.

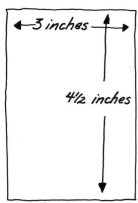

2.

4. Glue tracing paper on one end of the second roll.

5. Draw this bumblebee shape on cardboard.

6. Glue tracing paper on the cutout places.

7. Glue roll number 2 onto the bottom of the bumblebee.

8. Now insert roll number 1 into roll number 2 and blow!

Cut out the insides to leave an outline shape as shown.

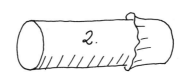

Stick 1 into 2.

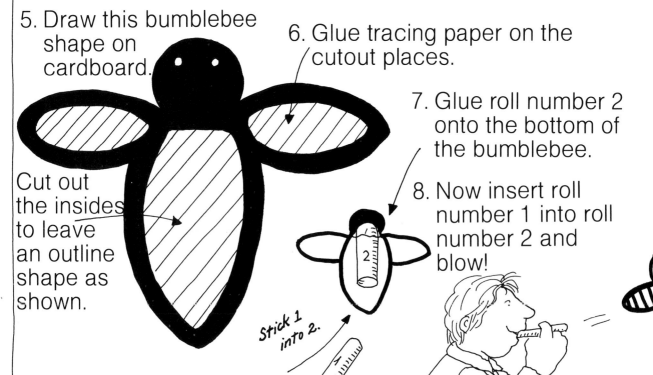

2

INDEX